A Sense of Detachment

A Sense of Detachment

JOHN OSBORNE

FABER AND FABER
3 Queen Square
London

First published in 1973
by Faber and Faber Limited
3 Queen Square London WC1
Printed in Great Britain by
Unwin Brothers Limited
Old Woking Surrey, GU22 9LH
All rights reserved

ISBN 0 571 10211 5 (hard bound edition)
ISBN 0571 10230 1 (paper covers)

All applications for professional and amateur
rights should be addressed to Margery Vosper
Ltd., 53a Shaftesbury Avenue, London W.1.

© John Osborne 1973

ACKNOWLEDGEMENTS

Acknowledgements are due as follows for permission to quote
from copyright material:

For 'Change Partners' by Irving Berlin, Irving Berlin Ltd.:
for 'In a Little Gypsy Tea-Room' by Joe Burke, Campbell,
Connolly & Co. Ltd.: for 'Booze, Twentieth Century Booze'
by Noël Coward; 'I'm on a See-Saw' by Vivian Ellis; 'Room
504' by George Posford; 'But Not for Me' by George
Gershwin; and 'Ev'ry Time We Say Goodbye' by Cole
Porter, Chappell & Co.: for 'Call Around Any Old Time',
'If You Were the Only Girl in the World', 'Goodnight',
'Yankee Doodle Boy' reproduced by permission of B. Feldman
& Co. Ltd., 64 Dean Street, London W1V 6AU: for 'The
Isle of Capri' by Wilhelm Grosz, Peter Maurice Music Co.
Ltd.: for 'Goodbye', 'Five O'Clock Shadow', 'Meditation on
the A30' and 'Ireland's Own' by John Betjeman, John
Murray (Publishers) Ltd.: for 'Jean' by Rod McKuen,
Twentieth Century Music Ltd.

The play was first performed at the Royal Court Theatre on
December 4th, 1972. The cast was as follows:

CHAIRMAN	Nigel Hawthorne
CHAP	John Standing
GIRL	Denise Coffey
OLDER LADY	Rachel Kempson
FATHER	Hugh Hastings
GRANDFATHER	Ralph Michael
SHIFTING PLANTED INTERRUPTER	Terence Frisby
SHIFTING PLANTED	
INTERRUPTER'S WIFE	Jeni Barnett
MAN IN STAGE BOX	David Hill
STAGE MANAGER	Peter Jolley

Directed by Frank Dunlop
Designed by Nadine Baylis
Lighting by Rory Dempster

CAST

CHAIRMAN

GRANDFATHER

OLDER LADY

FATHER

CHAP

GIRL

MAN IN STAGE BOX

SHIFTING PLANTED INTERRUPTER

SHIFTING PLANTED INTERRUPTER'S WIFE

STAGE MANAGER

Act One

The curtain rises on a virtually empty stage except for a projection screen at the back, a barrel organ downstage and an upright piano. After a slight pause, the principal actors walk on carrying light bentwood chairs. The actors are the CHAIRMAN, *a man in his mid-forties, the* CHAP, *who is slightly younger, the* GIRL, *who is younger still, the* FATHER, *who is about seventy, the* GRANDFATHER, *who is about ten years older and the* OLDER LADY, *who is about the same age. They place their chairs in position and look around them, at each other, the stage and all parts of the auditorium.*

CHAIRMAN: Well, this looks like a pretty unpromising opening.

CHAP: Blimey, you're telling me. The Stage Management look more interesting than we do. Or that lot out there. (*Indicates audience.*)

CHAIRMAN: Oh, dear, what does one expect?

CHAP: Nothing, I suppose.

CHAIRMAN: True.

(*The* CHAP *goes up to the projection screen.*)

CHAP: Oh, not one of *those.*

GIRL: I suppose you realize I haven't said anything yet?

CHAIRMAN: You will, you will.

CHAP: And paid for it.

GRANDFATHER: Overpaid, I expect.

CHAP: Right.

GIRL (*Points to barrel organ*): I hope no one's going to play that bloody thing. I can't stand barrel-organs.

CHAP: Oh, we'll have the bagpipes before we're finished, I expect.

GIRL: I can't stand the Scots either.

CHAP: I thought you were Scotch.

GIRL: Scots, you ignorant little bastard.

GRANDFATHER: Oh . . . is it going to be that sort of language?

GIRL: What sort of language?

CHAP: He means vaguely dirty, like we all use.

GRANDFATHER: I hope nobody's going to take all their bloody clothes off.

GIRL: Christ, so do I! All those limp, dangling dicks.

CHAP: And tits down to the knees.

OLDER LADY: Oh, I rather like all that.

GIRL: You would, you filthy old woman.

OLDER LADY: What did you say?

GIRL: You heard.

CHAP: Cloth ears. (*Points to* FATHER.) I hope this old sod isn't going to just sit there in his 1930's suit looking mysterious.

FATHER: I shall probably play the piano.

CHAP: You never played it very well.

GIRL: He's quite attractive.

CHAP: He's probably another 'exercise in nostalgia'.

GIRL: Oh, don't. Those boring T.V. chat shows!

CHAP: I shouldn't say that. You might find yourself on one.

GIRL: For what *they* pay?

CHAP: All you seem to do is talk about money.

GIRL: And why not? You don't think I get much from this bloody mean management, do you?

CHAP: Well, it's boring.

INTERRUPTER (*from stalls*): Hear, hear!

GIRL: Piss off!

GRANDFATHER: I may be old-fashioned . . .

GIRL: You are——

GRANDFATHER: But I still don't think young girls should talk like that.

CHAIRMAN: Not as old-fashioned as some of us.

INTERRUPTER: Dead right.

OLDER LADY: What did that man say?

GIRL: Some balls.

OLDER LADY: Who is he? Do we know him?

CHAP: Oh, I think he's *participating*, or something.

CHAIRMAN: No, just an obvious over-familiar theatrical device.

CHAP: Won't be the last one, either.

GRANDFATHER: Do you think we should offer him his money back?

GIRL: No, I don't!

CHAIRMAN: He's lucky to be here.

CHAP: *He* doesn't think so.

GIRL: He doesn't think anything just as long as he gets his salary at the end of the week. Can't wait for mine.

CHAP: Watch it. Or we may not be here tomorrow night at all.

GIRL: They've still got to give me two weeks' money.

CHAP: God, you are a Scot, aren't you?

CHAIRMAN: I don't think we should be nasty about the Scots. They'll think we've got it in for them, or something.

CHAP: Why not?

GIRL: Who cares?

CHAIRMAN: Exactly. Who cares?

GRANDFATHER: Good malt whisky.

GIRL: You're not going to burble on like that all the time, are you?

OLDER LADY: He's never been very interesting, I'm afraid.

CHAP: Ah, 'the theatre of antagonism'.

CHAIRMAN: The 'device of insult'.

GRANDFATHER: 'Oh, what a piece of work is Man . . .'

CHAP: Oh, belt up.

GIRL: I must say quoting Shakespeare is pretty cheap.

CHAIRMAN: Let's face it, it's all pretty cheap.

CHAP: *We're* pretty cheap.

GIRL: *I'm* not.

CHAP: Yes, we know about you. You're expensive.

GRANDFATHER: 'Oh, what a piece of work is Man . . .'

CHAP: Alas, poor old prick, I knew him well.

GRANDFATHER: How does it go on?

CHAP: 'A fellow of infinite jest, of most excellent fancy.' He has bored the arse off me a thousand times.

GIRL: Who?

CHAP (*in Shakespearean yokel type voice*): Why, he that is mad and sent into England!

GRANDFATHER: I suppose all life is a theatre.

CHAP: And all theatre is *laife*.

GIRL: What a profound insight!

CHAP: You mean *obvious*?

GIRL: Naturally.

INTERRUPTER: Is it all going to be as formless as this?

CHAIRMAN: Yes.

CHAP: I expect so.

GIRL: *You* try learning the bloody stuff. I've forgotten half of it already.

INTERRUPTER: You're trying to have it all ways, aren't you?

GIRL: As the actress said to the bishop.

INTERRUPTER: Do you think we can't see through this?

GRANDFATHER: I shouldn't think *he'll* sit through it.

GIRL: He will.

CHAP: We know, he's paid for it.

CHAIRMAN: Yes, I think we've had enough of him for a bit, don't you?

CHAP: Bit of your old Pirandello, like.

CHAIRMAN (*to* INTERRUPTER): Yes, I should go to the bar and have a drink.

GIRL: Don't think the Management will pay for it!

CHAP: I suppose *that's* a character trait, is it?

GIRL: What?

CHAIRMAN: Well, I suppose we'd better make some sort of start, though I don't know why.

GIRL: You either freeze to death or boil your knickers off.

INTERRUPTER (*walking out of auditorium*): Bloody right! Load of rubbish!

CHAP (*in pompous voice*): Hear, hear!

INTERRUPTER: My small boy could do better than this.

CHAP: Yes, I bet he likes small boys an' all.

> NOTE: *If there are any genuine interruptions from members of the audience at any time, and it would be a pity if there were not, the actors must naturally be prepared to deal with such a situation, preferably the CHAIRMAN, the CHAP or the GIRL.*
>
> *These can be obvious, inventive or spontaneous, apart from the obvious responses like 'Piss off', 'Get knotted', 'Go and fuck yourself if you can get it up, which I doubt from the look of you', etc.*

14

These could be adapted to the appearance or apparent background, like:

'*Get back off to the shires, you married pouve,*'
'*If you're Irish, get out of the parlour.*'
'*And I hope the ship goes down in Galway Bay.*'
'*Get back to Golders Green, you hairy git.*'
'*Why aren't you in the West End, watching some old tatty expensive shit?*'

Interrupter can return at any of these with any of the following abusive lines:

'*What we want is family entertainment.*'
'*When you've had a hard day's work, you don't want to sit and listen to a lot of pseudo-intellectual filth.*'
'*Bourgeois crap.*'
'*Do you expect to get the young people into the theatre this way?*'
'*Who cares about them? What about us?*'
'*All too obvious, I'm afraid.*'
'*Like it doesn't do anything for me, man.*'
'*I hope that the women are being paid the same as the men.*'
'*Like what's it all for, man?*'
'*They did all this in the 1930's, only better.*'
'*I'm glad I haven't got any money in the show.*'
And so on.

CHAIRMAN: Now where were we?
GIRL: Nowhere.
CHAP: Absobloodylutely nowhere.
   (*From the loudspeakers comes the lush sound of the Adagietto from Mahler's Fifth. They all listen in silence for a while.*)
CHAIRMAN: Oh, I don't think we need *that*, do you?
CHAP: I don't know, I should think we probably do.
CHAIRMAN: Always used to sneer at it, I remember.
GIRL: Still do, some of them.
OLDER LADY: Rather good ballet music, don't you think?
CHAIRMAN: Oh Christ! (*to the* CHAP) Anyway, ask him to turn it down, will you?
FATHER: I can do a passable Melville Gideon.
GRANDFATHER: Now he really *was* good.

GIRL: Don't start yet.

CHAP: I like barrel organs.

CHAIRMAN: Yes, I know what you mean.

GIRL: Oh, do get on with it!

CHAP (to CHAIRMAN): Yes, you *are* the Chairman and she wants her pay packet.

GIRL: I'm just thinking about what I'm going to have to eat afterwards.

CHAIRMAN: Why should *I* be the Chairman?

CHAP: You know perfectly well.

GIRL: Yes.

CHAP: You're the best equipped academically, apart from which you're a brilliant promotionalist, an eyes upward grown-in Committee Man.

OLDER LADY: Very good actor too.

GIRL: What do you mean, good actor? He's a bloody amateur. Always has been. That's why people think he's so good.

CHAP: That's why he thinks he's so good too.

CHAIRMAN (*rising*): Well, if you're going to be like that . . .

CHAP: Of course we're going to be like that.

GIRL: Oh yes, don't be *faux naif*. Just get *on* with it.

CHAP: Oh, is that how you pronounce it?

GIRL: What?

CHAP: *Faux naif*, you avaricious little berk.

CHAIRMAN: *Right*, we'll start.

GIRL: Thank God for that. I'm hungry already.

CHAP: You would be.

CHAIRMAN (*addressing audience*): Er . . .

GIRL: Ladies and gentlemen!

CHAP: *That* lot?

CHAIRMAN: What else do I call them?

GIRL: Who cares?

CHAP: Perhaps some of them *are* ladies and gentlemen.

GIRL: I doubt it.

CHAIRMAN: Try not to be too censorious.

GIRL: I don't know what that means.

CHAP: Bitchy.

16

CHAIRMAN (*addressing audience again*): *Some* ladies and gentlemen and the rest . . .

(*There is an enormous commotion as the* MAN IN THE STAGE BOX *stumbles in noisily, looks around at the stage and leers drunkenly at the audience. He is wearing an enormous fake fur coat, a striped football scarf and cap*).

BOX MAN: What's all this then?

CHAIRMAN (*burying face in hands*): Oh no, not *that* old one!

CHAP: Yes, running short I'd say.

BOX MAN: Running short? *We've* been running short—all the brown ale we've had. Up Chelsea!

CHAP: And up you too!

GIRL: I never understand these gags. Exclusively male, I suppose.

CHAP (*in mock imitation of her*): Oh yes, I dare say that's *very* true. *Very* true. Exclusively male.

BOX MAN: What's *she* then? Women's Lib? (*Snorts at his own joke.*)

GIRL: I knew it was a mistake.

BOX MAN: It's a bloody mistake all right. Your mother's mistake!

GIRL (*to* CHAIRMAN): Such an amusing theatrical device.

BOX MAN: I'M IN THE WRONG BLEEDING THEATRE!

CHAIRMAN: We're all in the wrong bleeding theatre.

BOX MAN: Is this Drury Lane?

GIRL: No, and it's not *Fiddler on the Roof* either.

OLDER LADY: What did he say?

BOX MAN: *You* can drop 'em for a start!

OLDER LADY: I suppose you think I wouldn't?

BOX MAN: All right, don't bother. Is there a change of scenery?

CHAIRMAN: No, but I'm afraid there will probably be some music.

GIRL: If you can call a barrel organ music.

BOX MAN: Go on, Grandad, give us a tune!

GRANDFATHER: No respect left.

OLDER LADY: Why should they?

BOX MAN: I can't make head or tail of this lot.

GIRL: And you won't. No tits.

CHAP: Oh, he's not such a bad idea.

BOX MAN (*standing up and addressing the audience*): Well, if you're going to fuck the chicken, I'll dangle my balls in the pink blancmange.

GIRL: Now what's he talking about?

CHAP: Does it matter?

(*Enter from Dress Circle the* INTERRUPTER.

INTERRUPTER: Rubbish! I want my money back!

BOX MAN: Yes, well I'm going to go and have a slash.

GIRL: Yes, we know, after all that brown ale.

BOX MAN: Oh, I could do something for you, Daisy.

GIRL: My name's not Daisy and *you* couldn't.

(INTERRUPTER *disappears.*

GRANDFATHER *gets up slowly and plays the barrel organ gravely. The* BOX MAN *joins in with the song and encourages the audience to join him.*)

BOX MAN (*singing*):

I don't care who you are

Make yourself at home

Put your feet on the mantel shelf

Draw up a dolly and help yourself.

GRANDFATHER (*addressing* BOX MAN): Those are not the words.

BOX MAN: Well, you don't have to be like *that*! I've paid my money, haven't I?

GIRL: No.

BOX MAN: Listen, you don't have to get all toffee-nosed with *me*. Or any of these other good people. We *make* you, the likes of you. Mr. John Public, that's what we are. Mr. and Mrs. John Public.

GIRL: I hope you'll be very happy together.

BOX MAN: We are—what's wrong with that I'd like to know? It's all right for you lot, sitting down there, looking all pleased with yourselves, getting paid hundreds of pounds.

CHAP (*to* GIRL): There you are.

BOX MAN: Where would you *be*, I'd like to know——

GIRL: You're repeating yourself.

CHAP (*to* GIRL): So are you.

BOX MAN: Thank you, sir. Now you're a gentleman, I can see that.

GIRL: He can't even . . .

BOX MAN: That's enough of *your* lip. Don't think I wouldn't come down there and smack your bottom—*and* enjoy it!

GIRL: I've no doubt, you poor old thing.

18

BOX MAN: All I said was he was civil and a gentleman.

GIRL: He's no more of a gentleman than you are.

CHAP: Good.

BOX MAN: Like some of these people here tonight. Look at them. Beautifully dressed, attractive women, lot of respectable people out there, including some of your real clever ones.

GIRL: Who do you think he's talking about?

CHAIRMAN: Yes, well I think we've had enough of *that*, too.

BOX MAN: What's that?

CHAIRMAN: I suggest, sir, that you come back later.

GIRL: Oh, *no*, please!

BOX MAN: I don't care what you say, I've paid my money and I'm going out for a slash.

CHAP: Perhaps it's not such a bad idea.

(BOX MAN *stumbles out of stage box with maximum of noise and so on.*)

CHAIRMAN: Shall I sit in the middle?

CHAP: Lucky Pedro, in the middle again.

GIRL: I suppose that's another joke?

CHAP: Masculine.

(BOX MAN *returns noisily. Shouts down at the actors.*)

BOX MAN: That's not funny, old man! Give yourself a kick in the pants!

CHAP: He pinched that from Peter Nichols.

CHAIRMAN: Actually, *he* pinched it from George Doonan.

BOX MAN: You're all a bloody lot of thieves and robbers! (*Staggers out.*)

CHAIRMAN: Well, as you seem to have suggested that my personality is best suited to imposing some order on this chaos——

CHAP: Or chaos on this order.

GIRL: As the case may be——

CHAIRMAN: I shall try to make a beginning.

INTERRUPTER (*from auditorium*): And about time, I say!

CHAIRMAN: Of sorts. Well, ladies and gentlemen and so on. The programme first, I suppose . . . Overpriced, as usual. Full of useless information. Like what part of Buckinghamshire the actors live in, how many children they've got, what their hobbies are and the various undistinguished television series that they've appeared in. On the front, there's the title.

GIRL: Awful.

CHAIRMAN: Yes, I'm afraid *that* will have to be changed.

CHAP: Too late now.

GIRL: Actually, 'Too Late Now's not a bad title.

CHAP: It's too late all right.

GIRL: Wasn't there a song called 'Too Late Now'?

CHAP (*In T.V. Chat Show voice*): Ah yes, 'a rather predictable exercise in somewhat facile nostalgia'.

GIRL: Oh, do stop knocking everybody. Let him get on with it.

CHAP: You still won't get paid till Friday.

CHAIRMAN: As I was saying—what was I saying?

GIRL: The programme.

CHAIRMAN: Oh yes, well we've agreed that the title will have to be changed.

CHAP: The author's name is far too big.

CHAIRMAN: So is the director's, come to that.

CHAP: And who cares who *presented it*? What's that—just making a lot of 'phone calls, having long lunches and getting secretaries to do all the work.

GIRL: Don't talk to me about directors. If ever there was a bogus job, that's one all right.

CHAP: Just letting all the actors do the work, like finding where the doorknobs are, finding out what the play's about by getting up and doing it, while they tell you what a genius you are.

CHAIRMAN: I don't think that's entirely fair.

CHAP: Like doing Hamlet as a Pre-Raphaelite queen.

GRANDFATHER: I used to like the old musical comedies . . .

FATHER: And a good revue.

GIRL: Well, you ain't going to get it, either of you.

OLDER LADY: I quite like it when they take all their clothes off.

CHAIRMAN: I'm sorry, but shall I go on or not?

(BOX MAN *returns noisily*.)

BOX MAN: I suppose you went to Oxford and Cambridge.

CHAIRMAN: No, actually I was only at one of them. Oh, dear, I suppose one shouldn't be so rude.

BOX MAN: Toffee-nosed pouf! (*Goes out*.)

CHAIRMAN: I agree with you that I may be occasionally and unforgivably toffee-nosed, but I am not a pouf.

GIRL: Oh come off it—we all know about *you*.

CHAP: You either likes one thing or the other, that's what I always say.

BOX MAN: Hear, hear!

CHAIRMAN (*to* GIRL): If I may correct you, my dear—

GIRL: Oh now, he's *really* being the Chairman.

CHAIRMAN: Yes, as a matter of fact, I am, and I would point out to *you* that you are out of order.

BOX MAN: Hear, hear!

CHAIRMAN: You do not 'know all about me', as you put it, neither will you do so.

CHAP: I would like to support the Chairman on that.

GIRL: You would, but we'll have a right gusher of North Sea Gas out of you and your dreary life before this is over. I know that.

BOX MAN (*returning*): Do you want me to sort him out, Missus?

GIRL: No, just shut up.

CHAIRMAN (*to* BOX MAN): Did you have an enjoyable slash?

BOX MAN: Are you taking the mickey?

CHAIRMAN: No, I was asking what I thought was a friendly question.

BOX MAN: Well, I tell you, doesn't half pong in there!

CHAIRMAN: Yes, well I'm afraid we've been trying to put that right for years.

BOX MAN: When I think of what ordinary working-class people like me——

GIRL: You're not working-class, you're just a loud mouth.

CHAP: As well as pissed out of your arsehole.

GRANDFATHER: Oh dear, I wish you wouldn't.

OLDER LADY: I rather enjoy the freedom of expression of these young people.

GIRL: What do you mean young—he's middle-aged!

BOX MAN: When I think of what people like us, people like us who do a real job of work, not like you, *you've* never done a job of work . . .

GIRL: Piss off!

BOX MAN: . . . Pay for their seats with their hard-earned money, and don't you use that filthy language at *me*.

GIRL: Why not?

BOX MAN: Because you're an educated woman, and you ought to bleeding well know better.

GIRL: Well, I'm not educated and I don't know any better.

CHAIRMAN (to BOX MAN): I think you've made your point, sir.

BOX MAN: Sing us a song! Oh Christ, I've got to go back to that stinking hellhole again! (He blunders out.)

CHAP (sings):

'Oh God our help in ages past,
Our hope for years to come,
Our shelter from the stormy blast
(All join in)
And our eternal home.'

GIRL: Hymns!

CHAP: Sort of scraping the barrel.

CHAIRMAN: To get back to the agenda, if that's what you can call it—I think we have dealt or at least spent enough time on this dull programme, the cupidity of the author and director——

CHAP (at GIRL): And the actors.

CHAIRMAN: I will only add that as you will see, or have seen, or predicted, that this neither is nor was an entertainment——

CHAP (in American accent): Nor a significant contribution to the cultural life of Our Time.

GRANDFATHER: Try not to be too nasty about the Yankees.

CHAP: Very good to us during the war.

GIRL: Well, they won it, of course.

CHAP: Yes. Flooded us with food parcels and French letters.

GRANDFATHER: And after the war.

CHAP: That's right. Lease Lend.

GRANDFATHER: Easy to sneer.

CHAP: Quite right. At least they didn't have to 'Go In', like 'Going into Europe'.

(Stage lights flash out and either a still or film appears on the projection screen of Mr. Edward Heath, smiling and waving to the full blast of the last movement of Beethoven's Ninth. They all watch in silence for a few moments, then the picture goes out and the music stops.)

INTERRUPTER: Cheap!

CHAIRMAN: I quite agree with you, sir.

INTERRUPTER: He's doing a good job!

CHAIRMAN: I quite agree with you about the cheapness aesthetically.
  (BOX MAN *stumbles back*.)

BOX MAN: All right for him. What about the poor bloody workers!

GIRL (*to* CHAIRMAN): Can't you get rid of him? I thought you
  were supposed to have some sort of artistic responsibility
  or something.

BOX MAN (*shouting down at* GIRL): You know what *you* need,
  don't you?

GIRL: Don't tell me, I'll guess. Not that *you* could, anyway.

BOX MAN: I'll see you later.

GIRL: Not if I can help it.

BOX MAN: Here, where's the bar?

GIRL: Just leap over the edge of the box, and it's the first crawl
  to your left.

INTERRUPTER: I must say I quite agree! I could do with a good
  stiff one myself.

GIRL: It would be the first time.
  (*Both the* BOX MAN *and the* INTERRUPTER *leave*.)

CHAIRMAN: No, it's not a device I really approve of.

GIRL: I wish you'd shut up saying 'device'.

CHAP: Give him a chance.

FATHER: I can do Turner Layton doing 'Transatlantic Lullaby'.

CHAP: Later. I'm afraid he's not very good at it.

GIRL: I thought he was supposed to be dead or something artsy-
  craftsy. (*to* CHAIRMAN) Well, isn't he?

CHAIRMAN: Oh God, why did I agree to do it?

GIRL: Because you like pretending you don't enjoy it.

CHAIRMAN: Right. *That's* the programme. *I* am the Chairman.

GIRL: Big deal.

CHAIRMAN: This girl is a—girl, I suppose. She will—er—do her
  best——

GIRL: For the money I'm getting?

CHAIRMAN: To stylize, or give some sort of life to, the various
  personalities—female, I mean—who thread their way
  through one man's particular experience.

GIRL (*to* CHAP): That should send them to sleep all right.

CHAP: Are they awake?

CHAIRMAN: Authentic, but not over-explicit, of a man's lifetime.

GRANDFATHER: Twentieth century.

CHAP (*sings*):

Booze, twentieth century booze, You're getting me down.

OLDER LADY: Well, of course, I was born in the nineteenth century.

FATHER: I was born in 1900. That's the same age as the century.

GIRL: How utterly fascinating.

CHAP: What the Chairman really means is this young lady——

GIRL: Thanks.

CHAP: Will come on with a few bitchy imitations of people she
personally dislikes.

CHAIRMAN: *As* I was trying to say, I am the Chairman, he is
some Chap, she is some Girl, that's his Father.

CHAP: Died 1940.

FATHER: Taught myself to play by ear so I'm not very good.

CHAP: Oh, I like the way you used to do 'There's an Old
Fashioned House in an Old Fashioned Street'.

GIRL: I thought he was supposed to be dead.

CHAP: Like *you*.

(BOX MAN *returns*.)

BOX MAN: Come on then, let's put a bit of life into it then!

GIRL: *You* put a bit of life in it. You haven't done anything up
till now.

CHAIRMAN (*pointing to* GRANDFATHER): And this gentleman is this
chap's Grandfather. Except that he's alive still, and this
Chap's Father's dead. (*Pointing to* OLDER LADY.) As for this
lady, she appears to be quite attractive, but as for the rest,
I am not sure. At least, not yet.

CHAP (*to* audience): So sort that out on your tambourines.

BOX MAN: Jolly good!

INTERRUPTER: I suppose we needn't ask if there's a *plot* or not!

CHAIRMAN: Quite correct, sir, you need not. However, I dare say
we'll stick in some safe bit for the audiences, so that they can
delude themselves that there is some intention and continuity.

GIRL: Either way they won't know.

CHAIRMAN: Of course.

BOX MAN: Sing us a song!

INTERRUPTER: Well, I'm going to complain to the Manager!

GIRL: Good. You *do* that.

INTERRUPTER: What's more, I shall go and see my M.P.

CHAP: Some south-east Tory, or right-wing Labour time-server.

BOX MAN: What about the old-aged pensioners?

CHAP: *You* should get an old prick's pension.

BOX MAN: They told me it was a musical.

CHAP (*sings*):
 'I'm a Yankee Doodle Dandy . . .'

GIRL: There he goes again.

CHAP: 'A Yankee Doodle do or die . . .'
 (*All join in.*)
 'A real live nephew of my Uncle Sam,
 Born on the fourth of July!'
 (*During this, the Stars and Stripes flutter on the projection screen.*)

INTERRUPTER: Cheap!

BOX MAN: Mocking the poor bloody American flag now.

CHAP: We *can* mock the British one if you prefer.

CHAIRMAN: No, I don't think we do, do we?

INTERRUPTER: No, we don't.

BOX MAN: What about a SONG?
 (*The stage lights dim, a frozen waste appears on the projection screen to the lone soprano sound from Vaughan Williams's Symphonia Antarctica.*)
 I don't mean that sort of highbrow stuff.

INTERRUPTER: You don't call *that* highbrow, do you?

CHAIRMAN: No. Very middlebrow I'm afraid. (*to* CHAP) Ask the Stage Management, will you?
 (*Projection and music stops.*)

CHAIRMAN: Right, let's sing him a song then.
 (*They all line up and sing the following to the tune of* Widdicombe Fair

ALL:
 Harold Pinter, Harold Pinter,
 Lend me your grey mare,
 All along, down along, out along lea,
 For I want to go to
 Printing House Square,

25

With Arnold Wesker,
David Storey,
Edward Albee,
Must get in an American,
Charles Wood,
Charlie Farnsbarns,
Christopher Hampton,
Sammy Beckett,
Sammy Someone,
Edna O'Brien,
Because she's a Woman,
And we're in enough trouble already,
Old Uncle Sammy Beckett and all,
And old Sammy Beckett and all.
(*Repeat verse to a dance.*)

CHAP: Well, now *I'm* going for a slash.

CHAIRMAN: And *I'm* going for a drink.

OLDER LADY: Is this the interval?

GIRL: The interval? You must be joking!

GRANDFATHER: Oh, can we go now?

CHAIRMAN: Everyone's free to do as they wish.

(*On the projection screen, there is a picture of the
Trooping of the Colour. The men all stand up. Very brief, this.*)

CHAIRMAN (*to the* audience): That wasn't actually meant to be
disrespectful.

BOX MAN: Ha ha di bloody ha ha! Where's the bar?

GIRL: By the men's loo, you drunken oaf.

INTERRUPTER: Take it off!

CAST (*to* INTERRUPTER): You take yourself off.

(*They all turn and dance off to the tune of* The Laughing
Samba. *As the auditorium lights come up, the* CHAIRMAN
*returns and starts to turn the handle of the barrel organ which
plays* Roll out the Barrel. *He then signals to the prompt corner.
A* STAGE MANAGER *appears to take over the handle, the*
CHAIRMAN *looks at his watch and saunters off. After a few
moments, the* STAGE MANGER, *clearly bored by the barrel organ,
stops turning it, and goes off as well.*)

END OF ACT ONE

Act Two

As the audience returns, if indeed it does return, the house lights are up and an extremely loud Pop Group is blaring out over the loudspeakers, against the Pop Group's still photograph on the projection screen. On stage, the STAGE MANAGEMENT *and* STAGE HANDS *and so on are dancing, some in an off-hand and some in a rather demented manner. After a while, and the* STAGE MANAGER *will have to decide on this, when what is left of the house has got back in, some of them will look at their watches and start to wander off the stage.*

The BOX MAN *does his usual entrance, clutching a crate of brown ale, one bottle of which he is tippling. He smiles cheerily round at the audience, standing up and waving at them.*

BOX MAN: This sounds a bit more like it! I came here to be *entertained,* I don't know about you.

INTERRUPTER (*settling into his seat*): So did I. Doesn't seem very likely *now.* That Box Office Manager was quite insulting.

BOX MAN: Dead right, sonny boy! So he was to me. Right gaffer's man you've got in there. Boss's man. (*Shouting at the stage.*) Well, get on with it! (*Down to the* INTERRUPTER.) I complained about the toilet.

INTERRUPTER: Good . . . I've got a tube to catch.

BOX MAN: Never you mind, sonny boy. If it doesn't buck up a bit, we'll all have a few jars and a general piss up.
(*He smiles broadly around him*) O.K. ? (*He starts to sing.*)
Why are we waiting,
Why are we waiting . . .

INTERRUPTER (*joining in*):
Why are we waiting,
Oh why, oh why . . .

(STAGE MANAGER *appears.*)

STAGE MANAGER: That won't get you very far, you know.

BOX MAN: It won't get *you* any bloody far either, if you're not careful. Just get on with it. They burn down places like this, you know.

INTERRUPTER: Oh, I don't believe in violence. But I don't see why one should sit and be insulted. Quiet protest is quite sufficient.

STAGE MANAGER: All right. Start Dim.

(*He goes off, and the house lights do indeed start to dim as the* FATHER *enters and sits down at the piano. He starts playing and sings a snatch of* On The Isle Of Capri. *He then sings* In A Little Gypsy Tea-Room *as his son, the* CHAP, *enters. They sing together.*)

FATHER AND CHAP:

'In a little gypsy tea-room,
You stole my heart away,
It was in a little gypsy tea-room,
I fell in love one day . . .'

(GIRL *enters.*)

GIRL: And he's such a thumping cad . . .

(*The* CHAP *sings to his* FATHER'S *accompaniment, addressing himself to the* GIRL.)

CHAP:

'I am only a strolling vagabond,
So good night, pretty maiden, good night,
I am off to the hills and the valleys beyond,
Good night. . .'

INTERRUPTER: Joan Littlewood did this years ago.

CHAP: 'Good night . . .'

GIRL (*to* INTERRUPTER): Piss off.

BOX MAN: Yes, give the boy a chance.

CHAP:

'So good night, pretty maiden, good night.
I come from the hills,
And the valleys beyond,
So good night, pretty maiden, good night.'

GIRL: All right. That'll do. (*to* BOX MAN) *He's* no boy.

BOX MAN: I want to see Val Doonican.

CHAP: And the Black and White Minstrels.

GIRL: Oh, he'll black up for you if you like.

INTERRUPTER: I like something entertaining, but that leaves you with something to think about afterwards.

GIRL: Well, forget it.

(*During this exchange,* CHAIRMAN *enters and starts to sing, again to the* FATHER'S *accompaniment.*)

CHAIRMAN: 'Oh, my love is like a red, red rose . . .'

(*to audience*) Join in all you old folks—we still need your money while you're here—

GIRL: Oh, my God! *His* love!

CHAIRMAN: 'That's newly sprung in June . . .'

(*to audience*) And all you youngsters too, even if you can't remember the words. You'll be with us a bit longer if you're lucky.

BOX MAN: We don't want any of that modern rubbish.

GRANDFATHER: 'Everyone suddenly burst out singing . . .'

CHAIRMAN:

'Oh, my love is like the melody
That's sweetly played in tune . . .'.

(*to* GIRL): I do hope you're not going to be cheap and obvious about the Scots.

GIRL: I couldn't be bothered, actually.

(*She immediately dances to a number by the* Supremes *with the* CHAP. *This lasts as long as it will seem to hold.*)

(*to* CHAP): You're not very good, are you?

CHAP: No . . .

(*Once again, while this has been going on, the* GRANDFATHER *has entered and sat down on his chair.*

There is a silence, or if there isn't a silence, the actors will have to improvise. However, when the next stage is reached, GRANDFATHER *rises slowly and also sings.*)

GRANDFATHER:

'Rock of ages cleft for me,
Let me hide myself in thee,' (*etc.*)

CHAP: Very good.

GIRL: Of course he's good.

INTERRUPTER: 'Ancient and Modern' now, is it?

BOX MAN: Sounds *bloody* ancient to me. Who wants a brown ale?

CHAIRMAN (*to* BOX MAN): I shouldn't overplay it too much.

BOX MAN: Don't you get grotty with me! She's dead right.

(*Pointing at the* GIRL): You're just a moaning old posh-voiced pouf.

(OLDER LADY *enters.*)

Come on, darling, sing us a song, or show us your knickers.

OLDER LADY: I will if you like.

CHAIRMAN (*to* OLDER LADY): What *are* you going to do?

FATHER: *I* know.

(*He starts to sing as he plays the piano a fair pastiche of Jack Buchanan.*)

'Good night, Vienna,

You golden city of a thousand dreams . . .'

(*As he plays and sings, the* OLDER LADY *and the* GRANDFATHER *execute a very dashing tango together. The* BOX MAN *applauds at the end of it.*)

INTERRUPTER: God, how sentimental!

BOX MAN: Give the old bag a break, or I'll come down and give you a right duffing up.

OLDER LADY (*to* BOX MAN): Thank you very much.

(*The* FATHER *does his introduction to* If You were The Only Girl In The World *and* OLDER LADY *sings to the audience.*)

'If I were the only girl in the world,'

GRANDFATHER (*rising*):

'And I was the only boy,'

CHAP (*also rising and singing*):

'Nothing else would matter in the world today,'

GIRL (*rising and singing and taking the* CHAP'S *hand*):

'We would go on loving in the same old way.'

OLDER LADY, GRANDFATHER, CHAP AND GIRL (*all join hands and sing the rest of the chorus*):

. . .'If you were the only girl in the world

And I was the only boy.'

INTERRUPTER: Oh God, I can't stand any more of this.

BOX MAN: Bloody good.

(*The* CHAIRMAN *lifts his eyes to heaven or at least somewhere above his usual line of vision and addresses the* INTERRUPTER.)

CHAIRMAN: I think I really do have to agree with you this time.

INTERRUPTER: And so you should. (*He gets up and goes out.*)

BOX MAN: Piss off!

GIRL (*to* BOX MAN): Thank you, sir, she said.

BOX MAN: You know what *you* need.

GIRL: Yes, you told us all that before.

CHAIRMAN: Does anyone remember where we were?

GIRL: You must be mad.

(*The* BOX MAN *rises and sings.*)

BOX MAN:

'Oh, he's football crazy,

He's football mad,

Since he joined the local football club . . .'

CHAIRMAN: I know—'He's lost the wee bit of sense he had.'

GIRL: If I were a man, my balls would hurt.

CHAP: Well, thank God you're not.

CHAIRMAN: Anyway, it's 'footba' crazy', not 'foot*ball*'. Anyone
can see *you're* not a Scot.

BOX MAN: Show us your kilt! What's your tartan, then?
The Macpouves I suppose.

CHAIRMAN (*wearily*): I had an idea you were going to say that.

GIRL: We *all* had an idea he was going to say that.

CHAIRMAN: Yes, now this Chap was going to tell us about his life.

GIRL: That's what we're all afraid of.

CHAIRMAN: So, old um—

GIRL: Chap.

CHAIRMAN: I think the floor is what they call 'yours'.

BOX MAN: Give him a big hand! He's only just started. You
never know. You might see him on the telly one day.

GIRL: Best place for him.

CHAIRMAN: Hear, hear.

(*The* CHAP *goes over to his* FATHER *at the piano and puts his
arm round his shoulders.*)

CHAP: You needn't sit there all the time, you know.

FATHER: No, it's all right, I quite like sitting here.

GIRL: You've already said he's dead anyway.

GRANDFATHER: Missed the twentieth century. I didn't . . .

OLDER LADY: No, neither did I. I'm rather glad, aren't you?

CHAP: No.

BOX MAN: We shouldn't have missed *you*.

(*The* INTERRUPTER *appears from another part of the house.*)

INTERRUPTER: Yes, I'd like to know what you'd have done without decent dentists and anaesthetics. Can't see you biting on to a leather belt.

CHAP: Nor you, either.

BOX MAN: Let him say his piece. It's a free country.

CHAIRMAN: It's not a free country.

BOX MAN: It's not a free country.

CHAP: As I was about to say——

(*The* GIRL *goes into another* Supremes *type dance, the* CHAP *joins her. The music finishes suddenly.*)

CHAP (*to* GIRL): Finished?

GIRL. Yes. Do carry on.

CHAP: As I was saying——

BOX MAN: What was he saying? This brown ale they sold me in the bar tastes like old horse piss.

GIRL: How would you know?

CHAP: . . . I was born——

GIRL: That's a promising start.

CHAP: And original too.

CHAIRMAN: Oh, do stop it, the two of you. (*to the* CHAP) Do you think you could get on with it?

INTERRUPTER: What do you mean 'get on with it'? He hasn't started yet.

BOX MAN: Give the boy a chance.

(*The* CHAP *advances downstage and taking his time, he surveys the audience and addresses them.—If there is still any left.*)

CHAP:

The last time that I saw the King,
He did the most curious thing,
With a nonchalant flick,
He pulled out his dick,
And said: 'If I *play*, will you *sing*?'

INTERRUPTER: Filth!

GIRL: Just bloody boring.

BOX MAN: I was in my cradle when I heard that one.

GIRL: Cradles weren't invented when *you* were born.

CHAP: I am going to make a sort of shortish speech about my life and women.

GIRL: Wouldn't you guess?

BOX MAN: Why, I've had more——

CHAP: Yes, than hot dinners. Except my dinners were probably a bit hotter and slightly more interesting.

BOX MAN: I'll come down and sort you out too!

CHAP: No, you won't.

CHAIRMAN: Yes, he's quite right. You're just an underpaid——

GIRL: Overworked——

CHAIRMAN: Exactly. What was it?

GIRL: 'Device' is what you keep saying.

CHAP: Now the first girl I really remember lusting after——

GIRL: Wake me up when he's finished.

CHAP: Was actually a woman.

> (*They all change places and take up* T.V. Chat Show *poses.*)

I don't know *what* age she was really. She could have been twenty-one or thirty-one. All I remember is that she had a small boy called Malcolm about three years old, I should imagine, and a bit younger than me.

> (*The* CHAIRMAN *clears his throat and becomes the* INTERVIEWER *to all the others.*)

CHAIRMAN: Now, J. Waddington Smith, you've just come from this play tonight—Did you think it came off at all? Or would you call it a total disaster?

GRANDFATHER: Not a total disaster, no. On the other hand——

GIRL: On the other hand——

GRANDFATHER: I must confess it did have *some* enjoyable moments.

CHAP: Oh, say that would you?

OLDER LADY: I quite enjoyed it. But then I suppose I'm easily pleased.

GIRL: Oh no, you're not. You're the worst audience in the world.

CHAP: Usual easy obligatory cracks about critics.

OLDER LADY: Well, naturally.

GIRL (*fiddling with her hair*): But he really has got a bit too predictable now, hasn't he? (*to* CHAIRMAN): They are getting me fiddling with my hair in the intellectual winsome bit, aren't they?

CHAIRMAN: Yes, but I shouldn't worry about it too much. I've already told them that——

GIRL: Device——

CHAIRMAN: Up in the Box not to overdo it too much.

OLDER LADY: Quite right.

CHAIRMAN (*to the* CHAP): It struck me that there was a certain amount of strident waffle. What would you say to that?

CHAP: Oh, I agree. After all, there ought to be a bit more to it than that?

GIRL: Oughtn't there?

CHAIRMAN: I agree. Didn't there? What did you think about the devices?

CHAP: The theatrical ones, you mean?

GIRL: Well, we did go to the *theatre*, didn't we?

FATHER: What *is* all this?

CHAP: They call it television.

GIRL: Yes, you really died before all that.

CHAP: Lucky old bugger.

CHAIRMAN: We're having a 'lively intellectual confrontation'.

CHAP: 'Making the news'.

CHAIRMAN: Do you mind? 'The first with the news'. (*Rising*)
I think we've *done* this for the moment, anyway, don't you?

CHAP: Oh, yes.

(*They all change around seats with the* CHAP *now in the middle.*)
Oh, yes . . . The lady with the three year old boy.

GIRL: Malcolm.

INTERRUPTER: Why don't you give the *young* people a chance?

CHAP: Why don't you give *us* a chance?

BOX MAN: You take a chance, darling.

GIRL: Don't be disgusting.

CHAIRMAN: Why shouldn't he be? He's paid his money. As he says.

GIRL: I doubt it.

BOX MAN: And I want it back!

INTERRUPTER: So do I.

(*All sing the Stoke City football song* We'll Be With You,

34

which also plays over the loud speakers, led by the BOX MAN, *who twirls his scarf, etc., bawling, while some of the cast stand up to the Wembley type stadium sound.*)

CHAP: Well, to continue if that's possible——

CHAIRMAN: If anything's possible . . .

CHAP: There were the twins. One was called Gloria, I know. And I think the other was Pat. But Pat was the nice one, Gloria was the dirty one.

GIRL: Oh, yes.

CHAP: Then there was a younger, blonde fat one, but I don't remember her name. But I do think she was more sort of humiliating than the rest. Then there was my Auntie Viv. She had very dark, curly hair.

FATHER: I used to call her the Gypsy Queen.

CHAP: That's right. But she had a funny way with handling the children. And I remember she said to me, 'Don't lift your trousers'—we used to wear what were called 'short trousers' then—'when you go to the toilet'.

GIRL: Are you going to go on much longer?

CHAP: Then there was Arabella.

GIRL: Arabella!

CHAP: Yes. She was twenty-one and I was about ten.

GIRL: And you 'would have died for her'.

CHAP: Yes, I would have died for her. She had a young man, who was an old man of twenty-eight. And we all three of us used to go for walks on the Downs. In the fog with the destroyers wailing and the invisible convoys.

GIRL: How romantic.

CHAP: Not at all. He (*pointing to* FATHER) was dying of T.B.

GRANDFATHER: Oh well, they used to die of it then.

CHAP: Like *flies*, in my family. My sister went and my God, did I resent it. What she left *me* lumbered with.

GIRL: Next.

CHAP: Next? Oh yes. Then there was Betty. She was a Brown Owl. And then a strapping great Girl Guide. Christ, I was mad about *her*. I used to follow her down the streets from school—it was a state school I suppose you'd call it—and pretend I wasn't.

35

GIRL: What did she look like?

CHAP: Can't quite remember. But very dark blue eyes and hair—thick. Showed her legs off a lot but not too much.

GIRL: Very sensible. Next.

CHAP: There was somebody, I think she was called Audrey. She was a frightful bully and had a gang of boys mostly and used to sit on your head and try to suffocate you. Red hair, I think.

GIRL: Ginger minge in your nostrils. That must have been nice.

CHAP: Then there was Gladys.

GRANDFATHER: I used to know a Gladys.

GIRL: Who doesn't? What about her?

CHAP: Nothing much, really. She just said one day she'd only ever really liked me because I had wavy hair.

GIRL: How awful.

CHAP: I suppose it was fashionable at the time.

GIRL: Why does it have to *be about* anything?

CHAIRMAN: The Second World War . . .

GIRL: Vietnam . . .

CHAIRMAN: 'Luxuriantly bleak' I would say, wouldn't you?

CHAP: Yes, but 'martially lyrical'.

GIRL: Images! Who wants them? You can have them any old time.

OLDER LADY: I suppose it's all really just about things like music and fucking.

CHAIRMAN: Yes, but I suppose we've got to *discuss* it.

GIRL (*to* CHAP): Yes?

CHAP: I don't think I can.

GIRL: Oh, don't start blubbing, it's too early.

CHAIRMAN: Much too early.

CHAP: I can't go through the *whole* list.

GIRL: We're not asking you to. Next.

CHAP: Then there was Shirley and her sister.

GIRL: What about them?

CHAP: I just wonder what happened to them, that's all.

GIRL: Well, we all wonder that sort of thing.

CHAP: Shut up, you lousy bitch. I wouldn't tell you anyway.

GIRL: And then?

36

CHAP: Well, believe it or not, there was Fanny.

BOX MAN: Annie and Fanny!

CHAP: That's right. The Fan Dancer who fell down on her Fan.

BOX MAN: Do you know the one about the crocodile shoes?

GIRL: Yes.

OLDER LADY: Oh yes, *I've* heard that one. It's awfully good.

BOX MAN: Are you bloody sure you've heard it?

CHAIRMAN: Yes.

BOX MAN: I'll bet you don't know what it's——

CHAP: Yes. It's got *three* punch lines.

CHAIRMAN: Next.

CHAP: Then there was Rosemary.

GIRL (*to the* INTERRUPTER): There's Rosemary for *you*.

INTERRUPTER: We don't know who any of these people *are*. What they're *doing*. Where it's taking *place*. Or anything!

OLDER LADY: Give the boy a chance.

CHAP: What? Oh, Rosemary.

GIRL: Yes, Rosemary.

CHAP: Ah yes, well, she had the rags up all the time.

GRANDFATHER: Well, they can't help it, you know.

CHAIRMAN: Well, he's got a point there.

CHAP: No, but she had it all the bloody time. I mean like all over the graveyard in Norwich Cathedral.

GIRL: Norwich—you mean like——

CHAIRMAN Yes. (*wearily*) Knickers off ready when I come home.

CHAP: I mean, Women's *Insides*. I've been walled up in them and their despairs and agony ever since I can remember.

GIRL: Perhaps you should try it yourself.

CHAP: I'm not strong enough.

GIRL: No, you're not.

INTERRUPTER: I think this sort of talk is highly embarrassing. My own wife is in the audience and I may say that she is undergoing what I can only call to someone like you, an extremely difficult——

GIRL: Period——

INTERRUPTER: No. I would say more than that. Expected but dramatic experience in her life.

GIRL: You mean she's got the Hot Flushes?

CHAP: Well, let me tell you, mate, *I've* had them for forty years.

GIRL: And you look it . . . So we've got to Rosemary.

CHAIRMAN: Yes.

CHAP: Oh, I don't remember them. Then there was Jean, I suppose.

GIRL (*dances and sings*): 'Jean, Jean . . .'

BOX MAN: You'll get no awards for *this* lot.

CHAP: She was really good and big and well-stacked and knew how to——

GIRL: Get you on the job.

CHAP: Christ, I was only nineteen! I could do it *nine times* in the morning.

CHAIRMAN: Nine times. Could you really?

GIRL: There's not much impressive in that.

CHAP (*in bad Scots accent*): 'Oh, there's not much impressive in that'. We've all had *colds*.

GIRL: And then there are all those dreary wives of yours.

CHAP: That's right. Those dreary wives of mine . . . They all think I'm a pouve.

GIRL: I'm not surprised.

OLDER LADY: I don't think she should have said that to him.

GRANDFATHER: I don't know what they are talking about. *Any* of them.

CHAP: The first one was pretty good in the sack.

GIRL: So you keep telling us. She looks pretty awful *now*.

CHAP: My fault.

CHAIRMAN: I don't think I'm being compromising but——

GIRL: But——

CHAIRMAN: Well, I do feel, and I know you're going to yawn or laugh——

BOX MAN: Sing us a song!

CHAIRMAN: We will, my friend, I'm afraid we certainly will.

CHAP: Oh yes.

CHAIRMAN: But there are certain dark, painful places we shouldn't expose—for our own sakes and those of others.

CHAP: Actresses are pretty rotten lays.

GIRL: So are actors.

OLDER LADY: I've just been reading some material that's been sent to me.

GIRL: What's *she* on about?

OLDER LADY: They seem to call it pornographic. But it looks quite interesting to me.

GIRL: So it would, you dirty old bitch.

BOX MAN: I watch T.V. most nights of the week and all I can say is that the general standard of programmes is deplorable.

CHAP: Say that again.

BOX MAN: Deplorable.

CHAP: That's better.

OLDER LADY (*reading from brochure*): 'This month we've got "The Virgin Bride was to be Raped".' How *fascinating*. 'This is the lead novelette. Then after "The Letters to Lucille"——'

GIRL: Who's Lucille?

OLDER LADY: I don't quite know. It doesn't say. But it goes on: 'We have a picture story about what a released convict is going to do to the first woman he sees when he gets out.'

BOX MAN: Come on, let's have a bit of *that*, then.

OLDER LADY: 'Next comes Part Two of "Sex in a Scout Camp". After that, Part Two of a novelette called "Young Orgy".'

BOX MAN: Get in there, it's your birthday.

CHAIRMAN (*despairingly*): We really do have to get rid of him, don't we? I mean we *are* all *agreed*?

INTERRUPTER: Get rid of the lot of you, *I* say.

OLDER LADY (*reading*): 'Then we finish with a girl masturbating herself in both her holes at one time.'

BOX MAN: Brown ale, anybody?

(*The lights dim and on the projection screen appears a column of marching British sailors. In the meantime, on the loudspeaker, the Band of the Royal Marines plays* A Life on the Ocean Waves, *naturally, at full blast. The* BOX MAN *joins in. When this has finished, the* CHAIRMAN *speaks, as do the others, and the same ritual is repeated more or less after each piece of so-called pornography is gravely but interestedly intoned by the* OLDER LADY.)

CHAIRMAN:

'Oh wad some Pow'r the giftie gie us,
To see oursels as others see us!

It wad frae mony a blunder free us,
And foolish notion.'

CHAP:

'Oh England, full of sin, but most of sloth;
Spit out thy phlegm, and fill thy breast with glory.'

GIRL:

'Love is a circle that doth restless move
In the same sweet eternity of love.'

CHAP (*at* GIRL):

'I do love, I know not what;
Sometimes this, and sometimes that.'

GRANDFATHER:

'Some days before death
When food's tasting sour on my tongue,
Cigarettes long abandoned,
Disgusting now even champagne;
When I'm sweating a lot
From the strain on a last bit of lung
And lust has gone out
Leaving only the things of the brain;
More worthless than ever
Will seem all the songs I have sung,
More harmless the prods of the prigs,
Remoter the pain,
More futile the Lord Civil Servant——'

CHAIRMAN: I think that perhaps at this stage we should say something else.

INTERRUPTER: You're telling us!

CHAIRMAN: Yes, well, you *may* have your chance later, my friend.
'I see phantoms of hatred and of the Heart's
Fullness and of the Coming Emptiness.'
(*The* CHAIRMAN *comes downstage and addresses everyone*):
Yes, just wait a moment.
'I turn away and shut the door, and on the stair
Wonder how many times I could have proved my worth
In something that all others understand or share;
But oh! ambitious heart, had such a proof drawn forth
A company of friends, a conscience set at ease,

It had but made us pine the more. The abstract joy,
The half-read wisdom of demonic images,
Suffice the ageing man as once the growing boy.'

BOX MAN: We don't wish——

CHAIRMAN: No, my friend, and you may well be right. But we
are all plagiarists, as even you. As Brecht said once and
Shakespeare better than us all.

GIRL: He's getting quite good, isn't he?

OLDER LADY (*reading again*): ' "Waterloo Bridge". The classic story
as in the film of a young girl met and seduced by an officer
during the Blitz of London. She gets fucked in a bomb
shelter while sitting beside some people that take no
notice——'

CHAP: Take no notice?

GIRL: Well, I suppose it's sort of sophisticated.

OLDER LADY: 'Then when he leaves her, she meets a lesbian who
puts her on the street as a "brass nail".'

GIRL: What's a brass nail?

CHAP: Don't ask me, I'm only here for the beer.

BOX MAN: Ha ha dibloody ha ha! Taking the piss out of us little
people again.

(*On the projection screen an image of a shy and beautiful
Edwardian girl. From the loudspeakers the sweet draining
sound of the soprano in Handel's* The Ode to Saint Cecilia's
Day.)

'But oh, what art can teach,
What human voice can reach,
The sacred organ's praise.'

CHAIRMAN:
'Now we maun totter down, John,
And hand in hand we'll go,
And sleep thegither at the foot, John Anderson, my jo.'

GIRL: 'Men are suspicious; prone to discontent; . . .'

CHAIRMAN: 'Subjects still loathe the present Government.'

GRANDFATHER:
'This is the time of day when the weight of bedclothes
Is harder to bear than a sharp incision of steel.
The endless anonymous croak of a cheap transistor

41

Intensifies the lonely terror I feel.'

(*The* CHAP *goes over to his* FATHER *at the piano*.)

CHAP (*gently*): Come and sit down. It's all over for *you*.

GRANDFATHER: Well, it was all over for him thirty years ago.

FATHER (*allowing himself to be led to a chair*): I am as old as the century.

GIRL: So you say.

OLDER LADY (*reading*): 'Number 53. Did you ever fancy getting hold of a pretty young girl-scout and fucking her up the arse-hole? Well, the two lucky lads in this picture story did just that. You see this lovely young girl was canvassing through their apartment block while they were in the process of screwing this girl, from both front and back. Well, when the girl-scout rang their bell they got the girl to get dressed and coax her in; once they got her inside they stripped her and gave her such a fucking she'll never forget it. Both of them get up her tiny little arse-hole. GREAT.'
(*On the projection screen, a scene from the final ensemble of* Der Rosenkavalier, *the sweeping melody for the* Marschallin, *and so on*)
'Hab mirs gelobt, ihn lieb—zu haben.'

CHAIRMAN:
'She is a winsome wee thing,
She is a handsome wee thing,
She is a lo'esome wee thing.
This sweet wee wife of mine.'

BOX MAN: Nancy Gobble Job, you mean!

GIRL (*to the* CHAP):
'Give me a kiss, and to that kiss a score;
Then to that twenty, add a hundred more:
A thousand to that hundred: so kiss on,
To make that thousand up a million.
Treble that million, and when that is done,
Let's kiss afresh, as when we first begun.'

CHAP: Oh, shut up, you silly bitch.

OLDER LADY (*reading*): 'A picture story of hard rape! Six men drinking in a small bar in Germany decide to grab the pretty little blonde barmaid and have a giggle with her but,

42

as many things do, it went wrong. She resisted! They
ganged up on her and tore her clothes off of her and
proceeded to violate her in every way that they could. Each
one had a go at fucking her, some in her bum, some in her
mouth. They held her on the table and screwed until she
finally passed out from the spunk forced down her throat.
I have seen some rape scenes while I have been in this
business, but *WOW*.'

CHAIRMAN: 'Tho' poor in gear, we're rich in love.'

CHAP:

'Bid me to live, and I will live
Thy Protestant to be: . . .'

BOX MAN: Watch it, you've got some of your bleeding Catholics
out here!

CHAIRMAN: Just ignore him.

CHAP:

'Or bid me love, and I will give
A loving heart to thee.
A heart as soft, a heart as kind,
A heart as sound and free
As in the whole world thou canst find,
That heart I'll give to thee.'

GIRL:

'My true love hath my heart and I have his,
By just exchange one for the other giv'n;
I hold his dear, and mine he cannot miss,
There never was a better bargain driv'n.'

GRANDFATHER:

' "O words are lightly spoken"
Said Pearse to Connolly,
"Maybe a breath of politic words
Has withered our Rose Tree;
Or maybe but a wind that blows
Across the bitter sea." '

OLDER LADY: 'Homo Action No. 5. As the cover picture shows
we have found a young man who is double jointed enough
to suck his own cock whilst he is being fucked by a big prick.'
(*On the projection screen a large rose.*)

CHAIRMAN: I suppose they'll play something from 'Cosi fan Tutte' now.

(*Naturally, the loudspeakers do.*)

GIRL: Of course.

CHAIRMAN: Well, I'll say this bit about the Rose anyway, and get it over with.

(*Fade music.*)

'And my fause lover stole my rose

But ah! he left the thorn wi' me.'

CHAP: Or, as he'd have said himself:

'Don't let the awkward squad fire over me.'

GRANDFATHER: I suppose it's all right. It seems a bit sad.

CHAP: Well at least you can't frighten the horses any longer.

OLDER LADY (*reading*): 'Free offer. Two young teen-age Sea Scouts are in the apartment of randy man; they were collecting for charity but they collected more than they bargained for. It didn't take him long to get their panties down and his big prick into their young mouths and cunts. Second No. 3. An efficiency expert comes into a humdrum office to get it running smoothly, then he gets the old maidenly book-keeper in and shows her how to fuck, when he gets them all at it he leaves. VERY FUNNY AND GOOD!'

(*The* FATHER *begins to play and* GRANDFATHER *stands up and sings.*)

GRANDFATHER:

'Life like an ever-rolling stream

Bears all its sons away.

They fly forgotten as a dream. . .'

(*All join in including* BOX MAN.)

ALL: 'Dies at the opening day.'

BOX MAN (*applauding himself as much as anybody*): That's a good one, that is.

INTERRUPTER: It's still filth and it always was.

(*Note: During the singing of the Hymn by the* GRANDFATHER *the projection screen shows an enormous ascending jet plane with the words 'If you want to get away, jet away'.*)

OLDER LADY: ' "Panther Kidnap." Two young members of the Black Panthers kidnap a white girl on the street and take her back to their pad. There they tear her clothes from her and make her perform all sorts of sexual perversions. She tries to fight them off but these two blacks are much too powerful for her. Lots of good action.'

(*The* FATHER *does another Jack Buchanan and sings a few bars of* Two Little Bluebirds.)

GIRL 'I dare not ask a kiss;
I dare not beg a smile;
Lest having that, or this,
I might grow proud the while.

No, no, the utmost share,
Of my desire shall be
Only to kiss that air,
That lately kissed thee.'

CHAIRMAN:
'Doubt you to whom my Muse these notes intendeth,
Which now to my breast o'ercharged to music lendeth?
To you, to you, all song of praises due;
Only in you my song begins and endeth.'

GIRL: 'Thy fair heart my heart enchained.'

CHAP: ' "Fool!" said my Muse, to me, "Look in thy heart and write." '

(*The stage lights dim a little while the loudspeakers play a few bars from* The Lark Ascending.
As the music ends abruptly, so do the lights come up and the OLDER LADY *continues with her next recitative.*)

OLDER LADY (*reading*): ' "Dog Scene." Not wishing to get into trouble with you animal lovers let me state right here, that although this is a very good action film with two girls a man and a dog it is by no means all action with the dog. He does, however, do a very good job of fucking both the girls then the man takes over for the screwing while the dog watches. A GOODY!'

(*On the projection screen a long view of a densely trafficked motorway. On the loudspeakers a few bars of 'Dorabella' from the* Enigma Variations.
Once again the music stops in almost mid bar as the lights snap on.)

45

GRANDFATHER:

> 'A man on his own in the car,
> Is revenging himself on his wife;
> He opens the throttle and bubbles with dottle
> And puffs at his pitiful life.
>
> "She's losing her looks very fast,
> She loses her temper all day;
> That lorry won't let me get past,
> This Mini is blocking my way.
>
> Why can't you step on it and shift her!
> I can't go on crawling like this!
> At breakfast she said that she wished I was dead——
> Thank heavens we don't have to kiss.
>
> I'd like a nice blonde on my knee
> And one who won't argue or nag.
> Who dares to come hooting at *me*?
> I only give way to a Jag." '

CHAP:

> 'Take thou of me smooth pillows, sweetest bed;
> A chamber deaf to noise and blind to light,
> A rosy garland and a weary head.'

OLDER LADY: "Anal Fuck." If you have ever had a snooty girl
working for YOU, perhaps you have felt like doing to her
what these two bosses did to this girl; after she had
destroyed several hours's hard work, they grabbed her and
tore her clothes off and while one fucked her in her cunt
the other stuck his prick up her arse. A very good film with
excellent colour work.'

(*During the* OLDER LADY'S *gentle declamation appears a fairly
pretty contemporary young girl on the projection screen.
Immediately this is finished, the loudspeakers play a few bars of*
The Nimrod *variation of Elgar. Stop.*)

CHAP:

> 'Her pretty feet
> Like snails did creep
> A little out, and then,
> As if they started at bo-Peep,
> Did soon draw in agen.'

CHAIRMAN:

> 'Bid me to weep, and I will weep,
> While I have eyes to see.
> Bid me despair, and I'll despair,
> Under that cypress tree;
> Or bid me die, and I will dare
> E'en Death, to die for thee.'

CHAP:

> 'Thou art my life, my love, my heart,
> The very eyes of me:
> And hast command of every part,
> To live and die for thee.'

OLDER LADY (*reading*):

> ' "The Diver." Skindiving enthusiasts will like this approach.
> Two girls bathing on a lonely beach suddenly find that they
> are being observed from beneath by a diver with an aqua-
> lung. He takes off one of the girls' bras and chases her up
> the beach for her pants; the other girl tries to help but she
> is soon stripped as well. Then lots of fucking. GREAT.'
> (*During this sequence*, SKINDIVERS, *male and female, appear on
> the projection screen.*)

BOX MAN: I know where I'm going for *my* holidays next year.

CHAIRMAN: 'That sweet enemy, France.'

CHAP:

> 'They love indeed who quake to say they love.
> Oh heav'nly fool, thy most kiss-worthy face
> Anger invests with such lovely grace,
> That Anger's self I needs must kiss again.'

OLD LADY (*reading*): This one's called 'Straight Wife Swap'.
(*On projection screen lone piper in kilt, possibly Ghurka.
Plays* The Flowers of the Forest.)

INTERRUPTER (*as lights snap back on*): What's all this thing about
the Scots?

CHAIRMAN:

> 'No! The lough and the mountain, the ruins and rain
> And purple blue distances bound your demesne,
> For the tunes to the elegant measures you trod
> Have chords of deep longing for Ireland and God.'

INTERRUPTER: Is this *ever* going to end?

BOX MAN: Sing us another song!

> (*The stage lights darken and on the projection screen a picture of miners emerging from the pit appears. On the loudspeakers is played* Cwm Rhondda.
>
> *The entire cast on stage stands with the exception of the* GIRL.
>
> *However, the* BOX MAN *stands up as reverently as he can with a bottle of beer to his lips.*)

INTERRUPTER: Oh, it's the *Welsh* now, is it?

GIRL (*to* BOX MAN): What are you standing up for? You're not even Welsh.

BOX MAN: No, but they're the best rugby players we've got.

CHAIRMAN: Have you ever watched rugby?

BOX MAN: No, have you?

CHAIRMAN: No, but I went to Rugby school.

GIRL: You would.

BOX MAN: Up Chelsea!

OLDER LADY (*reading*): 'A very good yarn about straight sex, lesbianism, feminine domination and flagellation.'

> (*On screen, a picture of a young couple kissing one another, somewhat chastely, but with undoubted passion. During this, the* FATHER *plays on the piano and sings.*)

FATHER:

> 'I like a nice cup of tea in the morning
> And a nice cup of tea with my tea,
> And at half past eleven
> My idea of heaven is a nice cup of tea.'

CHAIRMAN (*singing*):

> 'And when it's time for bed,
> There's a lot to be said
> For a nice cup of tea!'

BOX MAN: 'For a nice cup of tea!'

> (*He downs some more brown ale.*)

CHAP:

> 'Leave me, O love, which reacheth but to dust;
> And thou, my mind, aspire to higher things;
> Grown rich in that which never taketh rust;
> Whatever fades, but fading pleasure brings.'

GRANDFATHER: 'Never love was so abused.'
    (*to himself*) I seem to remember that somewhere . . .
GIRL (*to* CHAP):
    'O fair! O sweet! When I do look on thee,
    In whom all joys so well agree, . . .'
CHAP: Lying bitch!
GIRL: Yes!
    'Heart and soul do sing in me,
    Just accord all music makes.'
OLDER LADY (*reading*): ' "The Rustlers" '! This one appears to be,
    what does it say, oh yes, 'lesbian and straight, this story is
    about cowboys'.
    (*On the screen a picture of blind and gassed British soldiers
    from the First World War. The music is* The British Grenadiers.
    After the usual harsh snap-out the GRANDFATHER *rises again
    and talks almost to himself.*)
GRANDFATHER: It was seven-thirty a.m. on July 1st, 1916. That's
    when we went over the top.
INTERRUPTER: Yes, we know all that, 'sixty thousand casualties
    and two for every yard of the front'.
CHAP: Not bad for all that.
GRANDFATHER: More like the end, if you like to say so.
CHAP: Obvious.
CHAIRMAN: True, nonetheless.
BOX MAN: We don't want to hear all about that.
CHAIRMAN: I think that's pretty clear.
FATHER (*sings*):
    'I'm on a see-saw;' 'Room 504,'
OLDER LADY (*reads again*): ' "Slave Girl." Two stories of
    whipping, spanking and sex.'
GIRL: 'Won't you change partners and dance . . .'
    (*They all sit and listen rather dejectedly to* Variations on a
    Theme of Thomas Tallis, *at some time during which the*
    BOX MAN, *in a fit of generosity, starts to throw down bottles of
    brown ale to the* CHAIRMAN, *who distributes them among the
    actors and actresses.*)
BOX MAN: Here, have a drink on me.

(*to the audience*) Well, what are you all doing? Just fuck all.
I think they *need* a drink.

INTERRUPTER: *We* need something.

GIRL: We all do.

CHAP: I do . . . If I don't get it soon, I'll go potty.

GRANDFATHER (*to* BOX MAN): Your very good health, sir.

(*All the* ACTORS *on the stage rise and toast the* BOX MAN.)

BOX MAN: Jolly good luck. What about a bit more of that stuff?

CHAP (*sings*):
'They're writing songs of love,
But not for me.'

GIRL (*sings*):
'Every time we say goodbye,
I die a little . . .'

OLDER LADY: Yes, of course. Where are my glasses?

BOX MAN: Someone kindly give this old lady her glasses.

(*The* CHAP *does so.*)

OLDER LADY (*reads*): 'In time with the heaving of her own hips,
Miss Twitch moderately beat the youth's bottom. The
movement of her body increased——'

GIRL: Well, it would——

OLDER LADY: '——increased in its intensity with the strapping until
she stiffened and sighed.' I think *this* one's rather dull. It just
says 'Two Stories of whipping, spanking and sex.'

BOX MAN: Nothing wrong with that. Takes all sorts, you know.

CHAIRMAN (*leaning over to* OLDER LADY): May I have a quick
butchers?

OLDER LADY: Of course. My eyes are getting tired anyway.

GIRL: I was just hoping he wouldn't use rhyming slang. It's so
fatiguing to listen to.

(CHAIRMAN *reads from the piece of paper.*)

CHAIRMAN (*reading*): ' "To Each His Own. He paused, waiting,
and—sure enough, as with his finger Robin's bottom
accepted this new degree of dilation; and the lad relaxed—
so that he could thrust again—and force half the length . . .
Another gasp and a temporary tensing resulted from this
thrust—but this sudden clenching of Robin's rectum only
added to the thrills that David was getting from the opening

50

of this virginal bottom." *HOMOSEXUAL WITH A TINY BIT OF 'BI'.'*

INTERRUPTER: Some of us, you know, did go out at the time and try and do something about all that and it did get done, like it or not.

BOX MAN: Quite right.

CHAP: Some of your best friends are pouves.

INTERRUPTER: And it ill behoves——

GIRL: I do like 'it ill behoves'.

CHAP: Not bad.

GIRL (*to* INTERRUPTER): Shut up, revue artist.

CHAP: Bullshit artist.

    'Too long a sarifice
    Can make a stone of the heart.
    O when may it suffice?
    That is Heaven's part, our part
    To murmur name upon name——'

GRANDFATHER:

    'They must to keep their certainty accuse
    All that are different of a base intent;
    Pull down established honour; hawk for news
    Whatever their loose fantasy invent
    And murmured with bated breath, as though
    The abounding gutter had been Helicon
    Or calumny a song.   How can they know
    Truth flourishes where the student's lamp has shone,
    And there alone, that have no solitude?
    So the crowd come they care not what may come.
    They have loud music, hope every day renewed
    And heartier loves; that lamp is from the tomb.'

CHAIRMAN: I think we're mostly agreed about that.

INTERRUPTER: We most certainly are not.

BOX MAN: Give him another drink.

    (*He throws down another bottle of beer to the* CHAIRMAN *who does his best to catch it skilfully.*)

CHAIRMAN: Thank you.

    (*As he drinks from the bottle, the Union Jack appears on the screen and the loudest, most rousing version is heard of Blake's* Jerusalem.)

INTERRUPTER: Oh God!

(*He groans and moves off to the bar. The music snaps off again and the* CHAIRMAN *addresses the audience.*)

CHAIRMAN: Well, it's a sort of agreement.

'No, no, not night but death;
Was it needless death after all?'

CHAP: Cheers.

BOX MAN: God bless you. Is that *poetry*? Or just *talking*?

CHAIRMAN: Just talking.

'For England may keep faith
For all that is done and said.'

BOX MAN: Don't you worry. I *said* it was the World Cup this time. And I'll take on anybody!

CHAIRMAN:

'We know their dream; enough
To know they dreamed and are dead;
And what if excess of love
Bewildered them till they died?'

CHAP: Just a minute before you sit down.

(*He hails the* STAGE MANAGER *and he and the* CHAIRMAN *help to wheel on a pulpit. As they do so, the panatrope plays the Prisoners' song 'Durch Nacht Zum Licht' from Fidelio. As soon as the pulpit is in place, the music stops, the* STAGE MANAGER *goes off and the* CHAP *addresses the* GIRL.)

CHAP: You, I think.

GIRL: Oh no, you. I can't do imitations.

CHAP: Well, you *can*, actually. Impressions, really. Which are much better. However——

(*He ascends the pulpit and addresses the theatre in a thick Belfast accent. As he does so, the projection screen shows a group of extremely tough looking British troops in flak kit and riot masks, etc., facing a crowd of Irish civilians. L.C.*)

And I say to you, the British people, and by that I mean the people of Northern Ireland, that not only myself but all decent proper-thinking people throughout the world, whether Protestant or Catholic, are shocked daily and troubled by the tragic sight of our troops who must be the best, as well as the most disciplined in the world, being

incited physically, to say nothing of them morally and
spiritually, of seeing them, having to stand inactive
behind their shields while a lot of ignorant thugs
and hooligans are pelting at them with their bombs and
guns!

INTERRUPTER: There should be an Independent Inquiry.

BOX MAN: Quite right. Bloody hooligans.

GIRL (*turning on audience*): Murdering British soldiers, they're all
bloody murderers! You're all bloody murderers.

BOX MAN: Why don't you get back to Ireland and let us
unemployed British get on with the job!?

GIRL: Who needs England?

BOX MAN: *You* do for a start.

CHAP (*descending from the pulpit*): Right. Someone else carry on.
I was running out of steam anyway.

GIRL: That was clear.
(*The* CHAP *assists the* GIRL *into the pulpit. During this, the
Irish tricolour waves on the screen to an appropriate Gallic
tune. The* GIRL *addresses the audience from the pulpit.*)

GIRL: You all know what I think——

BOX MAN: I should say we do, we've heard it enough times.

GIRL: Well, it needs repeating to get into concrete skulls like
yours. Get out of Ireland!

BOX MAN: Get out of England!

GIRL: Don't think I won't!

BOX MAN: Good!

GIRL: You've oppressed us for three centuries.

BOX MAN: What about it? Bloody idle lot. Think you're all poets
and dreamers, I know. Shall I tell you something, mate?
The only thing that ever came out of Ireland——

GIRL: I know, is horses and writers.

BOX MAN: And who said that?

GIRL: A lot of Horse Protestants. And I'll bet you didn't know
who said that.

BOX MAN: Some bloody Catholic I.R.A. man.

GIRL: You're damn right.

BOX MAN: Well, I bet he did a damn sight better in London than
in Dublin.

GIRL: You're right——

BOX MAN: Do you want a brown ale? Of course I suppose you only drink bleeding Guinness.

GIRL: Stick your brown ale.

BOX MAN: And you stick your Guinness, and I hope——

GIRL: 'The ship goes down in Galway Bay.' That's the way with the lot of you.

CHAIRMAN: Oh dear, would anyone else like to say something?

INTERRUPTER: Yes.

BOX MAN: Shut your gob.

CHAIRMAN: Well, we do at least know that *that's* an Irish expression.

INTERRUPTER: I think it's all very well——

BOX MAN: Taking the piss out of the Irish——

INTERRUPTER: If you like. But what I object to, and I don't just say this on behalf of my wife——

GIRL (*descending from pulpit*): You wouldn't.

INTERRUPTER: But, as I was going to say before you interrupted me, all these jibes about bigotry are all very well but personally I find the implicit condescension inherent——

CHAP: Inherent!

INTERRUPTER: Yes, sir, inherent. It's a perfectly proper word and expresses what I mean to say.

CHAP: Which is——?

INTERRUPTER: That using a woman——

CHAP: As an object? Or were you going to say stereotype?

INTERRUPTER: Simply that you are being snide and coarse at the expense of a great many highly able and misused Women. Fortunately, you will no longer be able to get away with it.

CHAP: I didn't think I *had* got away with it. Perhaps I didn't try hard enough.

OLDER LADY: I quite agree with that gentleman. He is rather bad-mannered and silly, but, in this case, I think he's quite right. (*to the* CHAIRMAN): May I say a few words?

CHAIRMAN: By all means do. *You'll* probably say something sensible.

OLDER LADY: Thank you. (*She has already ascended the pulpit.*) May I say first that I have no particular personal complaint. In some ways, I was born into a good time.

54

And because of my natural intelligence, have managed to cope with what to most *men* would be an intolerable situation. My young friend here has complained, if I heard him correctly, of one of his earlier girlfriends being sick in the grounds of Norwich Cathedral. However, I would just say to him and others like him that it is a mere fact of life that women at all times and at all ages have suffered from, and in many cases died from, not merely childbirth but from what you would no doubt call the inbuilt tedium of organs such as the cervix, the vulvae, the vagina and the womb.

BOX MAN: Disgusting.

OLDER LADY: If men had to undergo what they so cheerfully call 'the curse'——

BOX MAN: Period pains——

OLDER LADY: ——They would have long ago invented some alleviation.

BOX MAN: Invent it yourself. Sing us a song.

OLDER LADY: I'm afraid our young friend here has let him delude himself into dreaming about something he thinks of as 'Eternal Woman'.

BOX MAN: Who doesn't?

OLDER LADY: That is because she is only valued by the excitement she may or may not arouse.

BOX MAN: Get off out of it, you old bag.

OLDER LADY: In short, she has to be desirable.

BOX MAN: Well, it does help, lady.

OLDER LADY: In the case of men, it appears not to be necessary. We women can be put down, if that is the expression, by the flimsiest physical or intellectual failing. We have been eternally abandoned from the Old Testament onwards.
All I say to you now is that we may all probably totally abandon you. Men, I mean.

(*She turns to the* CHAP, *who applauds.*)

OLDER LADY: Would you mind?

CHAP: Certainly.

(*He assists her down the steps although she seems to be in no real need of it.*)
My turn.

55

CHAIRMAN: Hurry it up a bit.

CHAP: Right ho, squire.

The nude is female by definition. Nudity is evasive, fleeing from description, allusive . . .

(*During this speech, various classic female nudes appear on the screen.*)

The naked male may be powerful, even beautiful, but self-defining like a jet aircraft in flight. Seldom is it more than technology made Flesh. Female, in this sense, is Art. The Male is Critic. Or, so it seems to me at this moment. Female is Art, secretive even when it conceals nothing. Revealing all, it is no sphinx for nothing, it contains and sustains life itself, taming random seed and even time. Making mystery of woman, the liberationists would say, is to belittle her in a glib religious conspiracy of fake mystery. Imprison her with the useful poetry of femininity and you destroy her in a cloud of voracious male imagination and inevitable social enslavement. The course of history! Woman is dead! Long live Woman! . . .

I do not believe it. She has always triumphed in *my* small corner of spirit, just as I have failed *her* image—my broken, misty, self-deceiving image you may say—during most of my life. And, remembering it, what a long time it has been. I believe in Woman, whatever that may be, just as I believe in God, because they were both invented by man. If I am their inventor, they are my creators, and they will continue to exist. During most of my life. What made me think of it? Watching a couple in a street late at night in a provincial town. Being in love, how many times and over such a period. Being in Love! What anathema to the Sexual Militant, the wicked interest on free capital.

Anathema because it involves waste, exploitation of resources, sacrifice, unplanned expenditure, both sides sitting down together in unequal desolation. *This* is the market place I have known and wandered in almost as long as I indecently remember or came to forget. Being in love, quaint expense of spirit, long over-ripe for the bulldozer; of negotiating from the strength of unmanning women's

liberation. Those long-shore bullies with bale hooks in bras
and trousers seamed with slogans and demands . . . Being in
love. Desolation in the sea of hope itself. Sentimental? False?
Infantile? Possibly. And infantile because my memories of
the phenomenon, if there be such a one, is or ever will be,
start so *young*. From three, yes, I know it was three, even till
the only twenty-one, there were so many girls, girl-women,
women of all ages, I loved. Very few of them were in love
with me, alas. Being in love blunders all negotiations and
certainly differentials. I have been sometimes indecently
moved to tears and if there were a court of justice in these
things, I would have been dealt with summarily as a
persistent offender, asking for innumerable, nameless and
unspeakable offences to be taken into account. However,
if I have been such a villain in this manor of feelings, I have
tried to be as clever as I know how. Knowing, as we all
know, that there is no such thing. If I have used blunt
instruments and sophisticated gear, I've tried to avoid soft
risks and only go for the big stuff. Naturally, I've made
mistakes. In fact, when you look at it, the successful jobs
have been far fewer than the fair cops. But that is the nature of
crime itself, of *being in love*; you are incapable of adding up
the obvious odds against you, unlike the law abider with
his common sense and ability to discriminate between his
own needs and that of the rest of society. To sustain and
endure beneath the law——

GIRL: *Beneath*, naturally——

CHAP: ——Being in love is a crime against women, and yes, oh
yes, reducing them to objects—as this splendid lady has
pointed out. To fantasies of poetry, poetry and piety and
bourgeois poetry, notwithstanding the workers at that.
It demeans men and serves their historic despotism,
whatever you think, over the female. So much is said; so let
it *be* so. It has not been the truth to *my* past; though it may
well be that of one who has been a truly conniving peasant
toiling under vicious and unnerving tyranny. The revolution
is about to break, comrades, and I for one shall not wait
to be explainable or forced heads down in the opening wave

57

of forced collective. *Girls past.* If I ever yearned for a
figment England, so I yearned for *them*; for girls past, fewer
in the present and sadly, probably in the future. Who *were*
they? All I remember most is their names, what they wore,
sometimes what they looked like. Not very much.

GIRL: You've said that about four hundred times.

CHAP: So I have. Yes. I have indeed . . .

(*He descends from the pulpit and he and the* GIRL *clasp each
other.*)

GIRL: Heart of my heart . . .

CHAP: Heart of *my* heart . . .

GIRL: People don't fall in love.

(*to audience*)

That idea is no longer effective in the context of modern
techniques. We are not nations or nation states. All that
must go. We are part of an efficient, maximum productive
ECONOMIC UNION. And Economic Unions do not fall in love.
They amalgamate. They cut down. They are NOW in the
Land's future. We are that Land and we are on the brink
of Progress. Even Progress has its cliché programmer.
But there. We have nothing but gain to contemplate. Loss,
such as it may have been, is, has been, ground into the
shining, kindly present even that is *ours* already! Even at
this moment. We are tearing down. We build! We build
now. And NOW.

We are not language. We are lingua. We do not love, eat
or cherish. We *exchange*. Oh yes: we talk. We have words,
rather: environment; pollution; problems; *issues*; oh, and——.
So century, century as is and will be—APPROCHE MOI!
Approche moi. To me . . .

(*The* GIRL *turns from the audience and kisses the* CHAP.)

CHAP: Oh, heart, dearest heart. What does *that* mean! Rhetoric.
I do, I have, I've wanted you, want you, will, *may* not and
so on. I love you, yes. I shall. Shan't. Heart . . . And I want,
yes—here we go—want to fuck you . . . Not cum-uppance
or any of that . . . Heart: I want you. Legs high. High.
Open. Prone: if you like. We can both laugh. And enjoy.
Enjoy me if you can. I *do* enjoy you. I *do*. I want you,

thighs enveloping my head. Mist. I shall want to breathe . . .
Give me *you*. I'll do what I can with me. I hate to use the
words between us—but—I want what I know, have known,
we know has taken, done, enjoyed, laughed over;
cherished. Between us. Girl. Chap. We are lost without . . .
You *know*. Don't you?

GIRL: Yes. I really think—perhaps—I do.

CHAP: Do. Don't. Will. Won't. Can. Can't. I wish I were *inside*
you. Now. At this moment . . . However.

GIRL: So do I. *However* . . .

BOX MAN: Very nicely expressed.

CHAIRMAN: What do you know about it?

BOX MAN: If I may be allowed to say so.

(*Everyone in the cast looks up at the* BOX MAN, *with the exception
of the* GIRL *and the* CHAP *who are intent upon each other.*)

CAST: Piss off.

CHAIRMAN: (*sings to the* FATHER'S *accompaniment*) My balls are
like a red, red rose.

BOX MAN: What time is it, for Christ's sake?

GIRL (*to the* CHAP): I've watched for you all my life.

CHAP: Likewise.

GIRL: And looked and wanted and as you would say, observed.

(BOX MAN *stands up and sings the opening bars of a patriotic
song. The auditorium is then almost bludgeoned by a recording
of the same song. After a few bars of this, the* CHAIRMAN
gets up, holding his bentwood chair.)

CHAIRMAN: Well, I think that'll have to do this time.

CHAP: It will.

CHAIRMAN: I'm not a good chairman at all.

INTERRUPTER: No!

CHAIRMAN: Very well, then——

(*He extends his hands to the rest of the cast and they all stand
hand in hand together and sing* Widdecombe Fair *in its
original. During the song they produce bunting with the words
on each piece* THE—VERY—BEST—OF—BRITISH—LUCK.)

CAST:

'Tom Pearce, Tom Pearce,
Come lend me your grey mare,

All along, down along, out along lea,
For I want to go to Widdecombe Fair
With Peter Davey,
Dan'l Widden . . .'
(*And so on.* CHAIRMAN *addresses the audience.*)

CHAIRMAN: So: that's what you'd call your lot. *Our* lot . . . And may the Good Lord bless you and keep you. Or God rot you.

(*All the* CAST *hum* When You Are Weary, Friend of Mine *as they pick up their chairs and go off, leaving the* GRANDFATHER, *who strums and sings* Old Father Thames. *He then goes off with his chair and the stage lights dim as one of the stage management comes on and idly turns the handle of the barrel organ.*

The cast return to face the audience but with no sense of 'Taking A Call'. The INTERRUPTER *boos and walks out, the* BOX MAN *applauds enthusiastically and drinks some more beer. The actors go off as the curtain falls.*)

THE END